The Black Country ... preserves and portray... ...ich history of the area for today's and future generations.

C000230437

The Black Country Museum was established in 1975 to collect, preserve, research and display items relating to the social and industrial history of the Black Country area and to arrange exhibitions, lectures, displays and publications. This included the construction of an industrial museum. The first buildings were moved to the museum in 1976 and since then the 26 acre (10.5ha) site has been developed to show a little of the unique living and working conditions of the Black Country.

In the many buildings on site, craftsmen and demonstrators re-create the activities of a time when the Black Country was the heart of industrial Britain. We hope that the fascinating history of the Black Country will come alive for you.

You will not find the area of the Black Country shown on any map. It is, however, that region of industrial activity, originally based on the mining of coal and the working of iron, which lies to the west of the City of Birmingham and straddles the ridge of hills running south east from Wolverhampton. It gained its name in the middle of the 19th century when thousands of furnaces and chimneys filled the air with smoke, and the mining of the coal, ironstone, fireclay and limestone turned the ground inside out, creating large expanses of dereliction. Beneath the Black Country lay the 'Staffordshire Thick Coal', a seam averaging 30ft (9m) in thickness and often only a few feet below the surface. The coal was extracted in great quantities and the ground above subsided dramatically. Large amounts of small coal left underground caused fires to transform vast tracts of the Black Country into a smoking wasteland.

In the 20th century mining ceased, but the reputation of the Black Country for the manufacture of metal goods still continues. This museum shows how people lived and worked in the area from the beginning of the 18th century to the present day.

RIGHT: *An artist's impression of the Black Country coalfields in the 19th century shows the large number of pit-frames in a small area. Horse 'gins', in the foreground, were used for winding coal up the shafts.*

BELOW: *Castlefields Ironworks is to be found in the centre of the museum Village. Approached along the cobbled Coppice Street, the Ironworks includes a Rolling Mill, Anchor Forge, and Chainshop.*

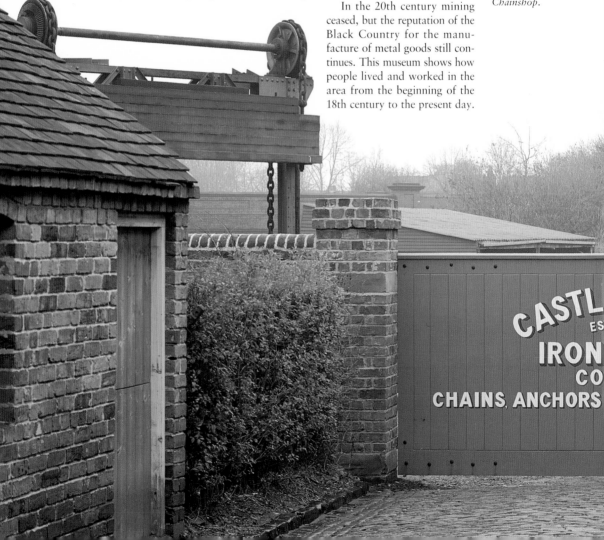

The Black Country Museum occupies a site of 26 acres (10.5ha) and is almost half a mile (800m) from north to south. This provides the opportunity to demonstrate many of the road transport exhibits which were both used and made in the Black Country.

An electric tramway system carries visitors from the entrance to the museum village and operates at the 3ft 6ins track gauge that was used throughout the area. The semi-rural nature of much of the route mirrors the Kinver Light Railway line which took thousands of Black Country men and women to the local beauty spot, Kinver Edge, before the days of mass car ownership and holidays abroad.

The museum tramcars have been saved from a variety of locations. The Dudley and Stourbridge single-deck No. 5, which was built in Tividale in 1920, was rescued from a garden in Kates Hill, Dudley, where it had stood as a summerhouse for 45 years after coming out of service in 1929. This single-deck four-wheel car is of the type designed for the Dudley and Stourbridge tramways in 1919 and built at both Tividale and at the Brush Works in Loughborough. A Brush-built car, No. 34, has also been restored. The museum's collection includes Wolverhampton No. 49, a Preston-built open-top double-deck car, and an early Wolverhampton and Dudley Tramway Company car which saw final service as Wolverhampton Works Car No. 19.

Electric tramcars were a common sight in the Black Country in the early years of the 20th century but the systems were replaced by electric trolleybuses or motorbuses by 1930. Some Birmingham tramcars continued running services to districts in the Black Country until the 1950s.

Trolleybuses first appeared on the Wolverhampton transport systems in 1927 and the Sunbeam Motor Company became a major manufacturer of such vehicles, continuing to produce trolleybuses until their final demise in the 1960s.

The Museum operates two trolley buses on a quarter mile (1200m) route around the site, the longest in Britain. No. 433 is a Wolverhampton 'W' built in 1946 for Wolverhampton Corporation. The original utility body was replaced in 1959 by a handsome one by Roe. The larger blue bus is No. 862 of Walsall's fleet. A Sunbeam of 1955 with a Willowbrook body, it was designed by Mr R. Edgley Cox, General Manager of Walsall Transport Department.

With its tradition of metalworking the Black

ABOVE: *Bean Long 14 motor car.*

LEFT: *Many people remember the green and cream trolleys running from Dudley to Wolverhampton in the 1960s. The blue trolleybus operated in Walsall.*

RIGHT: *Dudley and Stourbridge No. 5 tram.*

BELOW: *Bus stop.*

Country has been a centre for the manufacture of both components and complete motor vehicles since their inception. Companies such as AJS, Clyno, HRD, Rock, Bean, Star, Sunbeam, Guy, Thompson and Zenith produced complete vehicles and many of the axles, chassis and forged-metal parts used by the major manufacturers are still made in the Black Country. A 1925 Bean Long 14 and a 1931 Star Comet are the museum's examples of locally manufactured cars, and it is the museum's policy that motor vehicles, as with most exhibits, are operated regularly. The cars feature at rallies and road runs.

There are also horse-drawn delivery carts and travellers' wagons in the collection.

ABOVE: *The earliest known drawing of a Newcomen engine in operation, by Henry Beighton, 1717.*

BELOW: *Diagram showing how the Newcomen engine operates.*

In 1712 Thomas Newcomen built the first successful steam engine in the world, used for pumping water from coal-mines on Lord Dudley's Estates. In 1986, after more than ten years of painstaking research, the museum completed the construction of a full-scale working replica of that 1712 engine.

The 'Fire Engine', as it was known, is an impressive brick building from which a wooden beam projects through one wall. Rods hang from the outer end of the beam and operate the pumps at the bottom of a mine shaft which raise the water to the surface. The engine itself is simple, with only a boiler, a cylinder and piston, and operating valves.

A coal fire heats the water in the boiler, which is little more than a covered pan, and the steam generated then passes through a valve into the brass cylinder above the boiler. The cylinder is more than 7ft (2m) long and 21ins (52.5cm) in diameter. The steam in the cylinder is condensed by injecting cold water and the vacuum beneath the piston pulls the inner end of the beam down and causes the pumps to move.

The primary source of information for this replica was an engraving produced in 1719 by Thomas Barney of Wolverhampton. The material for the engine house and the individual parts of the engine were generously provided by many local organizations.

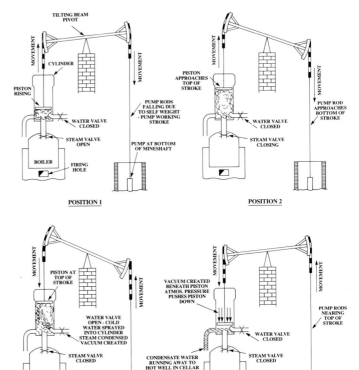

RIGHT: *The pit-frame at Racecourse Colliery is typical of those used in the Black Country. It is made of wood and could be moved to another shaft nearby rather than transport coal long distances underground.*

FAR LEFT: *The Newcomen engine at work. An engraving by Thomas Barney in 1719 showed Dudley Castle in the background and the engine house has been rebuilt in the same relative position today.*

BELOW: *The brick walls form the loading wharf from which the coal was transferred to the carts for distribution.*

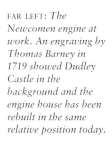

The ground beneath the museum site was once mined for coal, limestone, fireclay and ironstone. More than 40 old mine shafts are shown on old plans and around one of these shafts Racecourse Colliery has been built as a typical small Black Country coalpit.

The 'Thick Coal' seam was the greatest source of the coal mined in the Black Country but there were other, thinner, seams and from one pit shaft it was often possible to mine up to 40ft (12m) of coal, producing a theoretical yield of 50,000 tons per acre. This coal was often not more than a few feet below the surface. So much coal was easily accessible from one shaft that the pits had only simple winding engines and timber pit-frames. Racecourse Colliery has a single-cylinder steam winding engine, with the winding drum outside the building capable of serving two shafts, one for raising coal and the other for removing water. The layout is similar to that of many Black

Country pits and the engine was used at a pit in Amblecote, near Stourbridge.

The colliery is so named because the land on which it stands was originally the Dudley Racecourse which was closed when the railway line from Dudley to Wolverhampton was built in 1846.

Racecourse Colliery is shown as it would have been in about 1910 with the Manager's Office in the Weighbridge House from Rolfe Street in Smethwick and the typical Hovel and Blacksmith's Shop. The original shaft beneath the pit-frame was 120ft (37m) deep.

The narrow-gauge rail-tracks which are used to run the tubs from the pit head to the 'landsale wharf' or the spoil heap, also connect Racecourse Colliery with the Brook Pit to the south. This is also built over an original shaft and is typical of the small pits to be found in the 1930s when mining in the Black Country was in decline.

The Staffordshire Thick Coal was a seam of coal unique to the Black Country and at Foxyards in Tipton, only a mile or so from the museum, the coal seam was recorded as over 50ft (15m) thick. It was made up of several different seams, each with their own name and different physical characteristics, with almost no rock or 'partings' between them.

Thick Coal is still occasionally found when open-cast mining or when land reclamation works are carried out but it would be very difficult to take people into any Thick Coal workings today.

'Into the Thick' is an underground experience created by the Black Country Museum to show how miners worked the Thick Coal and other seams in the Black Country in about 1850. It is a drift mine, with a sloping tunnel down which you can walk into a maze of roadways and working areas so that you can experience the underground conditions in a safe yet realistic way.

RIGHT: *Sitting by the air door all day, young boys like Billy would often find the job cold and frightening.*

BELOW RIGHT: *'Holing Under'. Cutting away the bottom of the coal seam so that the rest might be allowed to fall or be prised down was one of the most skilled and dangerous jobs in a coal mine.*

BELOW: *Pit ponies were used to transport coal from the pit face to the shaft and the pony and its handler formed a special relationship working together underground.*

Once underground, in a timber-lined tunnel with the sound of water dripping from the roof, you meet 'lija Wedge, a miner of the 1850s, who leads you through the underground passages.

'lija explains how the mines were run and how timber pit-props were used to support the roof when coal was extracted or roadways developed; how boys like little 'Billy' started work at the age of 10 or 11, in a cold, damp job opening the air doors which directed the air around the pit to prevent gas collecting and causing explosions. The pit pony 'Sally' and her minder 'Matthew' are seen pulling a tub full of coal to the pit bottom, and at face in the Heathen seam the miner working beneath

LEFT: *The Thick Coal seam was unique to the Black Country, but the full 30ft (9m) thickness was not always mined at one time. This 'side of work' indicates how much coal there was underground and the way in which it was extracted.*

BELOW: *In the 1850s Black Country pits concentrated on producing large lumps of coal which were packed onto trolleys and held together with iron bands for transporting to the pit bottom and then to the surface.*

the coal, cutting with only a pick, emphasizes the danger and hard work of mining in the days before mechanization.

The sound and shake of blasting at the rock face and the roar as tons of coal fall from the roof are further reminders of the dangers faced by the miners. At the pit bottom 'lija tells of the number of deaths caused by accidents which happened in the shafts and explains why 'rattle chain', which was used to lift the coal to the surface, was so called. The chain was made up of three separate chains held together with timber pegs and was a good deal safer than a simple link-chain or rope.

The roadway from the pit bottom is cut through the 'Thick Coal' and leads to a 'side of work' where the size of the working area is awe inspiring. In such a workplace when the coal was dropped from the roof as much as 300 tons could fall to the ground at a time – not a place to linger for too long and yet 'lija and his workmates are seen eating their lunch while Isiah Turner is working on the coal far above their heads.

Coal mining was a dangerous business, and the high accident rate in the mid 19th century, particularly in the Black Country, led directly to the setting up of the Mining Commission and laws to improve safety.

LEFT: *The tilted cottage is one of the collection of buildings from throughout the Black Country that has been dismantled and relocated at the museum.*

BELOW: *The Toll House, just across the road from 'Jerushah', the tilted cottage, has not yet suffered from mining subsidence.*

At the top of the site, next to the tram and trolleybus terminal, stand a pair of Cast Iron Houses. They were constructed when devastation of the Great War had left a shortage of skilled builders and an increased demand for council housing. They were originally situated on the Birmingham New Road and were constructed by bolting cast iron plates together which, although quick and easy, proved costly. The rent was therefore expensive at 10 to 12 shillings, which most people could not afford. Completed in 1925, first choice of renting was given to those who had served in the forces and their families. The houses were occupied until September 1987, when asbestos was uncovered and health inspectors insisted the houses should be pulled down.

Close to the Racecourse Colliery are three small cottages. The tilted cottage 'Jerushah' is a vivid reminder of the effects of subsidence. It was carefully dismantled and rebuilt exactly as it was found in Gornal. The position of each brick in this building was carefully recorded before it was dismantled and it was then rebuilt exactly on its present site to show the effects of this subsidence. This cottage was one of a number built in Coopers Bank, Gornal, on a piece of land made available by the Earl of Dudley's Estates. In 1881 the cottage was occupied by Benjamin Meredith and his family and by 1910 Joseph Bradley was the occupier. Jerushah Bradley, his daughter-in-law, lived in the house until 1984 and the cottage is named after her.

Across the road from 'Jerushah' is a small single-storey cottage which was originally built in Bilston close to Alfred Hickman's Ironworks. The cottage was probably built by Sam Pitt with his own labour, and it is of very simple construction.

On the other side of the road is a Toll House, which dates from 1845 when the Sedgley to Tividale Turnpike road was built. Its original location was in Woodsetton, about

three miles from the museum, and it only operated as a Toll House for about 20 years. There would have been a gate across the roadway outside the cottage and all travellers and animals would have been charged for using the road.

ABOVE: *The simplicity of the furnishings in the Toll House bedroom indicates the relative poverty of the house's occupants.*

LEFT: *The small windows on the front of the Toll House would have been used to watch for approaching traffic. The tramcar operated long after the toll gate had been removed but the windows still provide an opportunity to see what is going on.*

RIGHT: *A domestic scene of the 1920s in the back room of No. 12 Brook Street. The kitchen range and fire surround are similar to those found in displays of an earlier period but the gas cooker is a modern addition and reflects the wealthier nature of the house's occupants.*

RIGHT: *Even the kitchen furniture at No. 12 Brook Street is up to date. This labour-saving unit has an integral flour canister and shopping list.*

The interior of the cottage is now displayed as it was in about 1920 when it was occupied by widow Anne Hodgkiss and her daughter Lilian. Many of the items on display came from the family and their photographs are on the walls.

No. 12 Brook Street, in the centre of the museum village down by the canal, was occupied by Joseph Nicholls and shows the home of a fairly prosperous person. Records in 1924 show him as an 'art metal worker' and the quality of the furnishings and fittings indicate his greater wealth. The house was one of three in a block built in Brook Street, Woodsetton, near Sedgley, in about 1852.

From the front there appear to be two houses but there are, in fact, three. No. 10, on the left, has only one room and a pantry downstairs and there is a similar house at the back. Such back-to-backs were a feature of the Black Country with rows of four, six or eight being common. No. 11, the rear house, is displayed as if occupied by a veteran of the First World War who works in the brass foundry in the yard behind the building. The year is 1924 and the family, with a small child, is quite poor.

The other house in the block, No. 12, is a 'through house' with a comfortable front room, complete with wind-up gramophone. The kitchen has such luxuries as a gas cooker and a 'Hygena' kitchen unit. The staircase to the two bedrooms is reached through the door by the side of the fireplace.

At the rear of the house the brewhouse, or brew'us, had a glazed passage connecting it to the house, a refinement added in the early 1920s and used by the occupant in Woodsetton as a place to grow tomatoes. Nos. 10 and 11 shared a small brew'us and toilet, which is a Day's 'tippler', patented in 1884.

LEFT: *The Chain-maker's House in Canal Street was built some 30 years later than the Brook Street Cottages, but this interior dates from 1910 and the fittings have changed little since the house was built. The bottle jack, a vertical rotating spit, that hangs over the fire is one of the few luxuries owned by the Chainmaker, who would have worked in the oddwork shop at the bottom of the garden.*

Canal Street runs through the centre of the village and many of the buildings were originally built as houses. The Sweet Shop, Baker's and Pawnbroker's were first built before 1850 but most of those on the other side of the road date from 1879.

The General Store, Gregory's, was built in Old Hill in 1883. A pair of houses with a central entry, it was converted in about 1910 to enlarge the shop area and at that time the entry next to the canal was constructed.

Next to the General Store is the Chainmaker's House. This was moved from its original location at 91 Lawrence Lane, Old Hill, and it is typical of the many 'two up, two down' houses built in the area after the 1872 Housing Act. The Act laid down limits on the minimum size of rooms and you can see the difference between this building and Brook Street or the other cottages. The front room of the Chainmaker's House would not usually have been open to every visitor. It was reserved for important visitors or use on Sundays. Most of the life of the house would revolve around the black grate, or range, in the kitchen. Between the two rooms the stairs go down into a small cellar, or pantry, and the staircase to

the two bedrooms leads out of the kitchen.

In the back yard is the brewhouse, used for washing and baking, so called because of the practice of brewing beer in the boiler. By the end of the 19th century the design of terraced houses varied little across Britain, but a separate brewhouse and a workshop at the bottom of the garden were a particular feature of Black Country houses.

BELOW: *The parlour of the Chainmaker's House would only have been open to visitors on special occasions. The picture of Queen Victoria and her family would have been a prized possession even after the Queen's death.*

RIGHT: *The kitchen of No. 11 Brook Street, one of the back-to-back cottages, is occupied by a young family who must have found the space rather cramped.*

BELOW: *The typical Nailmaker's brewhouse was used for washing clothes and brewing beer. In the corner is the water boiler with the 'posser' or 'posher' on top, a manual forerunner to the washing machine.*

BELOW: *Cast-iron pump from No. 11 Brook Street. It was used to draw rainwater collected from the roof, stored in a cistern under the brewhouse.*

Next to the Bottle and Glass Inn is a pair of cottages which are replicas of 18th-century buildings in Old Hill. The museum was unable to find any early cottages of this type in the Black Country which could be moved to the site and these have been copied from a row in Station Road, near the entrance to the Gorsty Hill canal tunnel. They have been built to the details shown in a photograph about 1900.

Originally there were two small cottages, each with one room downstairs and one upstairs. The left-hand cottage had a parlour and brewhouse added in about 1860, with an additional bedroom, and the other was extended in about 1890. The Newton family, who had been nailmakers, owned the cottages at this time and Zeta Newton ran a small general store from what is today the Cobbler's Shop. The garden behind the cottages produced both flowers and vegetables for the family's needs.

Overlooking the Museum Village stands St James's School. First built in 1842 in Salop Street in Dudley, it was moved to the Museum in 1991, the work made possible by a generous grant from the Charles Hayward Trust. Today you can see how it would have been in 1912.

The school was built near St James's Church and was designed by the same architect, William Bourne of Dudley. A medallion struck in 1843 as a fund-raising venture for the school shows it with lancet windows and stone crosses on the roof.

The school was built to accommodate 300 children but probably never taught that many. It attracted children from three to seven years, but older children were far less likely to attend regularly in the last century as they could earn a living or help at home.

Originally boys over seven were taught in one part of the building and girls and infants in the other; in 1868 the two halves were amalgamated to form a Mixed School.

The school building suffered from poor natural lighting, bad ventilation and unsuitable heating, and by 1904 conditions were so bad that it was recommended that the school be closed. Dudley Education Committee was unwilling to close the school and in 1906 moved the Mixed School to St Thomas's while St James's continued as an Infants School only.

By 1912 it had been possible to make improvements to the school including new toilets, larger cloakrooms, a new partition and the fitting of larger windows, and the building looked much as it does today. It continued as a school until 1980 and then became a community centre until 1989.

ABOVE: *Children playing in the yard of St James's School.*

LEFT: *Seated on hard wooden benches children relive the schooldays of their grandparents.*

LEFT: *The Ark Speedway with its original high front boards waits to thrill children of all ages.*

The travelling fair, like the one by St James's school, brought entertainment to people a century or so ago. It would set up on a piece of waste ground and for a few days provide a range of thrills, entertainment and a change for those who might never go on holiday.

The Jones family of Cradley Heath started travelling with the fairs in the early 1900s. Today the fourth generation runs the fairground by the school. The traditional side shows of coconut shy, hall of mirrors and shooting stalls are next to the Cake Walk, Slip, Swingboats and Ark Speedway.

The Slip, or helter-skelter, was travelled by the Ayres family, before it came to the Museum. The Ark was the latest thing in high-speed rides when introduced in the 1920s. The Ark in the Museum fairground was built by Lakin of Streatham, London, in 1932 for the Townsend family who travelled it around the south of England. As with most fairground rides it was updated over the years but fortunately it was not converted into a waltzer and remains one of the few 'four lift' Arks in the country.

Fairgrounds were the first places in which most people could see moving pictures, before picture houses were built and halls used to show films. In 1921 a Black Country man from Brierley Hill, John Revill, built a small cinema on land adjacent to his house. Today the cinema has been rebuilt exactly as it was in 1926. It is tucked behind the Hardware Store, adjacent to the Bakery and Brass Foundry, and shows not only silent movies of the 1920s, but film of the Museum's industrial exhibits at work.

RIGHT: *Detail on the side of the Cake Walk, an almost-forgotten fairground ride, first imported from America.*

LEFT: *Just one half of Gregory's Store indicates the wide range of items for sale. Sweets and tobacco, crockery and drapery, compete for space with tea and dry goods, boots and childrens' clothing.*

BELOW: *Weighing sweets in Thomas Cook's sweetshop. The brass rollers mounted on the wall are used to form the different shapes of sweets in the machine on the bench.*

The museum Village has been built on the low ground at the northern end of the museum site which is surrounded on three sides by canals. To the north the Dudley Tunnel Branch is the canal which runs from the Birmingham Wolverhampton canal to the northern portal of the Dudley Canal Tunnel built in 1883. The southern boundary of the Village is a parallel canal arm built in 1840 to provide access to Lime Kilns which the Dudley Estates built to process limestone mined on the Castle Hill. The two arms were connected by a short branch formed, it is believed, by the subsidence of the ground caused by coal mining. The buildings within the Village, as well as with the whole museum, have been brought together from throughout the Black Country to save them from destruction and to create an urban landscape typical of the Black Country area.

These houses, shops, workshops and factories represent a cross-section of the social and industrial history of the Black Country.

Gregory's General Store stands next to Canal Street bridge which was erected in Wolverhampton in 1879. The bridge was threatened with demolition when the Wolverhampton Ring Road was being built, and it

LEFT: *Rolling pills in Emile Doo's Chemist's Shop is a fascinating job to watch. The shelves and bottles had remained untouched for many years when the museum collected them in the 1970s.*

BELOW: *The window display in the Haberdashery Shop changes with the season to show some of the clothing in the collections.*

was carefully dismantled and rebuilt at the museum to provide access to the Village area. The shop was built as a pair of houses and Mrs Gregory first started selling goods from one of the front rooms. As business developed the shop grew. In 1923 major alterations were made and the present shop front installed. Virtually everything required by the community in and around Lawrence Lane was stocked by the shop. Meat and dairy products were sold from the counter at the right-hand end, groceries and greengrocery from the centre and an unlikely combination of sweets and drapery from the left-hand end of the store.

Further down the road towards the Chapel is the Chemist's Shop. This is a replica of the shop run by Mr Harold Emile Doo in Halesowen Road, Netherton, whose family donated the fixtures and fittings when the shop closed in 1974. The Netherton shop was originally a tailor's, built in 1886, and Mr Doo, whose father James moved to the area from Cambridgeshire in 1882, moved into it from his premises on the other side of the road in 1929. He closed one shop at 10 p.m. on Saturday night and reopened for business in the new premises at 9 a.m. on Sunday morning.

In the centre of the Village, opposite the Pub and the Chapel, stands the Hardware and Ironmonger's Shop.

The building was erected at the junction of Pipers Row and Tower Street in Wolverhampton in 1827 and had a variety of uses before it was dismantled to make way for redevelopments in 1980. Today it houses the Ironmonger's in the corner shop and the Hardware Store in the larger unit that fronts onto Canal Street. The two separate shops are assumed to be in the same ownership, as was the case in Pipers Row, and the upper rooms are reached by a single staircase.

The corner unit is based on Nash's Ironmonger's Shop from Oldbury from where the shelves and many of the contents came. In the windows is a display of tools and equipment typical of the products of the ironworking manufacturers of the Black Country. In the Hardware Store you can see the tin baths and wire netting, enamelled-ware and lamps so often made in the Black Country, together with the wide range of domestic items which a hardware shop would have sold.

A traditional feature of the hardware shop was the practice of displaying the wares outside the building. The tin baths and wire netting were stacked on the pavement and the baths and buckets hung above the windows. Every morning the shop assistant had to set up the goods outside and clear them away at night. When it rained the buckets even had to be emptied of water to prevent them falling off the hooks.

Next to the building when it stood in Wolverhampton was a pair of small lock-up shops with a courtyard behind them.

BELOW: *The Hardware Store is an Aladdin's Cave of goods that were once an essential part of life, such as the wooden-rollered mangle, galvanized dustbins, paraffin heaters, bristle-brushes, carpet-beaters, and wicks for lamps – the list is almost endless.*

One of the two shops today situated between the Hardware Store and the Pawnbroker's is a Fried Fish Shop. The building is a replica copied from two shops in Lower Lichfield Street, Willenhall. The original shops were built as houses and converted to front room shops between 1900 and 1910 when they were used as a Grocer's, a Butcher's and a Fried Fish Shop from 1916 to 1932.

In 1994 the Museum collected the frying range and fittings from a fried fish shop in Old Birchills, Walsall, operated by Mrs May Lambourne and her husband between 1933 and 1954. Mrs Lambourne cooked and served in the shop while Mr Lambourne peeled the potatoes in the back yard and cleaned the fish in the kitchen. Originally the shop had a tiled window-back and customers could select the fish they wanted frying from those in the window. To conform to modern health and hygiene standards, the original frying range, made by Walker & Husler of Birmingham between 1926 and 1930, has been converted from coal-fired to gas.

The Pawnbroker's is in a pair of cottages which were rescued from Himley after they had been partially demolished by a runaway lorry. The front room of the shop was where unredeemed pledges or other lines could be bought, but if you wished to pawn, or 'hock', something you went into the panelled 'Pledge Room' at the back to obtain a little privacy.

The building next to the canal is based on the design of the shop in Birmingham Road, Oldbury, which was Frederick Veal's Bakers. The original building is still standing next to the line of the old canal loop and it has been altered many times. The Baker's Shop is a replica of Mr Veal's shop as it was in Oldbury in 1910, with wooden shelves and displays in the window. The shop sold not only bread products but also British wines, and customers in 1910 could have obtained a glass of wine with biscuits for threepence. The coal-fired bakery at the rear was saved from the site in Oldbury. Today it produces loaves for demonstration only, as modern health regulations prevent the bread being sold or even eaten.

The Sweet Shop was built in memory of Thomas Cook, a sweet-maker who lived in the Minories, Dudley, in the 1880s and who emigrated to America at the turn of the century. Sugar is boiled up in the back room, and then made into various shapes of sweets on the counter in the shop.

RIGHT: *The 'Gold Flake' advert on the outside of the building has been rebuilt exactly as it was, with every brick in its place.*

BELOW: *Nash's Ironmonger's in the corner shop would serve the variety of industries in the area. The tongs in the bucket might have been used in the Rolling Mill, and the boxes of nails and screws and the various tools used by the skilled craftsmen of the region.*

LEFT: *The inside of the Darby Hand Chapel reflects a simple austerity but the building comes to life with the services held in it.*

RIGHT: *Inside the 'Bottle and Glass', local real ale and a convivial host welcome today's visitors as much as yesterday's workers.*

BELOW RIGHT: *The 'Bottle and Glass' stands in the centre of the Village as a major landmark. The building originally had a much simpler frontage but the imposing façade was added in the 1870s.*

BELOW: *Children in costume leave the Chapel after an assembly service at the beginning of a visit to the museum.*

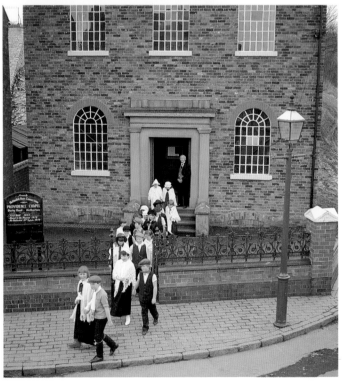

The Methodist Chapel was built in 1837 in Darby Hand, a part of Netherton in Dudley, and is typical of many such buildings to be found throughout the country. It was closed in 1974 and carefully dismantled to be rebuilt at the museum between 1977 and 1979.

The tiny settlement of Darby Hand grew up in the late 18th century as a coal-mining and nail-making community at the side of the Dudley Canal.

Some of its people are known to have come from Belper in Derbyshire. As early as the 1780s a family called Darby organized a Sunday School, which met in local houses. A plot of land in Northfield Road was purchased in about 1815 and Providence Chapel was opened 29 January 1837. The Chapel, with two out-buildings and a Sunday School in the basement, cost £950. It was affiliated to the Methodist New Connexion, which had broken away from the main Methodist body in 1797 and which was very strong in the Dudley area.

Services in the Chapel are arranged by the Friends of the Museum throughout the year, including a Sunday School Anniversary and Harvest Festival, helping to recreate an important aspect of Black Country life.

The 'Bottle and Glass' stood originally on Brierley Hill Road, Brockmoor, backing onto the canal at the 'Stourbridge Flight' of 16 locks. It was probably built shortly after the canal was cut. A map of 1822 shows 'The Bush' public house but by the 1840s it was known as the 'Bottle and Glass'.

The pub was built with two large rooms fronting the street, with the stairs in their present position in an extension at the rear. The back room was a later addition and the join between the two phases of construction can be clearly seen. The front of the pub was altered in the latter part of the 19th century, and the wooden seating and partitions date from these alterations. The corridor seems to have been formed in the 1870s.

Next to the pub is the Carter's Yard where working horses can be seen from time to time. It has a brick stable for two horses, a harness room and cart shed.

LEFT: *The Glasscutter at work in his workshop behind the General Store. The intaglio lathe he is using does not cut deeply into the glass and for larger crystal pieces he will use other machines in the shop.*

BELOW: *The Tub Shop, or Brass Foundry, is so called because the moulds into which the hot metal is poured are formed in the sand tub by the window. Here the caster is returning sand to the tub from around the horse brasses which he has just produced.*

Behind many of the houses in the Black Country could be found small workshops in which skilled craftsmen carried out their work. In the Village you can find a Glasscutter's, an Oddwork Shop, an Engineer's Shed and a Brassfounder's.

The Glasscutter's, behind Gregory's General Store, is based on one in Bridge Street, Wordsley. Small glasscutting workshops were found in many back gardens in the Stourbridge and Wordsley district although they would not usually house so many different machines. Two of these are wooden, deep-cutting lathes used to cut traditional designs into the crystal glass for which the area was famous. The smaller 'intaglio' lathe is used to decorate many simpler items.

At the rear of the Brook Street back-to-back houses stands a Brass Foundry which was originally built in 1869 in Shaw Street, Walsall. It would have been operated by two men, or casters, as they were known. Although it was more famous for the products of its ironworks, the Black Country produced many brass items, including lock parts and machinery bearings.

RIGHT: *The Office at the end of the Trap Shop is where the records of the company would have been kept and the wages made up. The small pots in the foreground are for the wages of the individual workmen.*

ABOVE: *The Trapworks is an almost Dickensian assembly of presses, forges, and machinery used to produce and assemble the many individual parts of the traps.*

The caster reproduces brass items from lead patterns by pouring molten brass into a sand mould produced by pressing the pattern into the sand. The moulds are prepared on the 'tub' by the window, which is full of the sand used, and brass is melted in a crucible in the furnace in the floor.

Sidebotham's Trap Works, between the Chapel and the canal, was moved to the museum from Wednesfield, near Wolverhampton, between 1982 and 1985 and is an example of a small factory in which animal traps were made. Wednesfield was a major centre for the manufacture of such traps and they were exported to many parts of the world. The stencils hanging from the roof were used to mark the packing cases and show the names of ports in Africa, South America and elsewhere.

The building is shorter than the original factory, but all the necessary machines have been installed from the Wednesfield works to enable traps to be made. The stamping, pressing and punching machines at the office end of the building are driven by lineshafting from a single-cylinder gas engine of 1906, built by Tangye's of Smethwick. The forge hearth was used to make the springs which operated the traps and the parts were assembled on the benches, using the hand-operated fly presses, before being painted or 'blacked' in tanks by the canalside wall and packed for delivery.

The strangely-named Oliver Shop has been built by the railway embankment near the Tilted Cottage. It was originally operated by T. W. Lench of Blackheath and, with its ten hearths, produced a variety of small forged items, including pipe clamps and special bolts.

The Black Country is renowned throughout the world for its production of iron and steel goods, including chains of all sizes, nails, tubes, forgings, rolled products and castings. In the Castlefields Ironworks many of the ironworking processes of the area can be found, and the Nailshop just outside the gate is a reminder of the earliest 'metal bashing' industry of the region.

The Nailshop is a replica of one built in about 1880 in Chapel Street, Halesowen, which was last worked by Mr Sidney Telfer in the 1940s. The building originally had four nailers working in it, two at each hearth using spring-pole operated hammers or 'Olivers'. As trade declined two of the Olivers were removed and an anvil installed in order that some general smithing could be carried out.

Nailmaking was well established in the Black Country by the Middle Ages, and at its peak in about 1820 there were over 50,000 nailers at work in and around the Black Country. As the trade in handmade nails declined due to the mechanization of the industry the Black Country turned to the production of chains for which it was to develop an international reputation. The Chain Shop in the Ironworks was built using two hearths from one of the last firms in the area to make handmade chain, Bloomers of Quarry Bank,

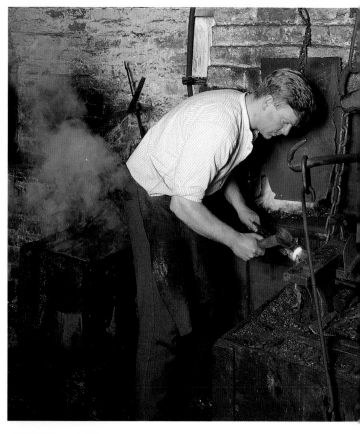

and a replica of one at Cruddas in Cradley Heath. The smaller hearths are set up to make chain with the iron about ½ in (12mm) in diameter, while the larger one would be used to produce heavier chain that required two men to make it.

Next to the Chain Shop, which is operated every day, is the Blacksmith's Shop with its 'Goliath' forging hammer used to produce tools and small forgings for the Rolling Mill and the restoration of many of the museum's exhibits. The equipment came from Eliza Tinsley's in Old Hill and the building, a former cottage which still has its fireplace and ceiling, was moved from Great Bridge.

The Rolling Mill in the large open-sided shed by the canal has been set up as a typical Black Country re-rolling mill in which iron or steel bars could be reduced in size or changed in section. The mill stands, the mangle-like machines through which the hot iron is passed, were donated by the British Steel Corporation from the Birchley Works in Oldbury, and the furnace in which the bars are heated is a replica

LEFT: *Making handmade chain in the Ironworks Chainshop. Black Country chains were renowned for their quality throughout the world.*

BELOW LEFT: *The Nailmaking Shop is today used to make special nails and spikes for boats being restored.*

RIGHT: *The Rolling Mill stands by the side of the canal and the furnace for heating the iron bars can be seen at the far end of the building. The Rolling Mill is used to produce special wrought-iron sections for conservation work.*

BELOW RIGHT: *The Office in the Ironworks includes templates for setting the Rolling Mill, business records and pattern books for the production of special items.*

using new parts which were specially cast for the job. Iron bars about 2¼ ins (57mm) square and 2ft (60cm) long are held in tongs and fed through spaces which reduce in size between the rolls, emerging smaller in cross-section and much longer.

The other large building in the Ironworks, with its cast-iron columns and wooden roof trusses, houses the Anchor Forge. The building was saved from Johnsons Rolling Mill site in West Bromwich, and the forge hammer and furnace were rescued from Isaïah Preston's in Cradley Heath where the hammer was installed in the 1920s to forge parts for ships' anchors. The furnace is similar to the one in the Rolling Mill, but the iron billets heated in it are much larger and are suspended from a crane in order that they can be manipulated beneath the steam-powered hammer. The heat from the furnace also raises steam in the boiler between the furnace and the brick chimney and this steam powers the hammer to reduce the size of the iron and forge it into the shape required.

The Village is surrounded on three sides by canal. To the north the Dudley Tunnel Branch runs past the 'Bottle and Glass' to the tunnel portal from where electric narrow boats operated by Dudley Canal Trust run into the spectacular caverns. To the south the Lord Ward's Arm, built in 1840 to provide access to the limekilns, originally extended for half a mile (800m) to meet the Old Main Line from Wolverhampton to Birmingham. To the east the branch by the Boatdock was formed by mining subsidence in the middle of the 19th century. Lord Ward's Arm is now cut off where it runs under the Birmingham New Road and a Wharf Boat, a 90ft (27m) long timber boat which could only be used on the Wolverhampton level, lies across the old junction.

The Lifting Bridge between the Ironworks and the Boatdock was built across the railway transhipment basin at Lloyds Proving House near Factory Junction in Tipton. Huge weights hanging on chains over the four pulleys balance the weight of the roadway, and the deck can be raised and lowered by operating a small hand-winch.

The Boatdock is typical of the many built on the Black Country canals. Three boats can be drawn out of the water sideways, and the dock is fully equipped to build new working craft and repair those of iron or composite construction. The main buildings are a blacksmith's shop, nail store, rivet store, paint store, timber shed stable and tackle store. Of these only the blacksmith's is of brick. The remainder are made up largely of old boat timbers, the front wall of the nail store and rivet store being the bottom of a boat with doors and windows cut through the timber.

The canal around the Village is used as moorings for a variety of privately owned traditional boats, and those on view change from week to week. The *Diamond*, a Midlands and Coast Canal Carrying Company boat which was built in 1927, rests on the dock allowing you to see inside the tiny living cabin. *Diamond* worked between the Black Country and the ports of the Mersey estuary, but the other unpowered, or Butty, boats are typical Day Boats which worked behind a horse or tug in and around the Black Country. The steam narrow boat *President* is jointly owned by the museum and Dudley MBC and makes regular trips around the English canal system.

ABOVE: *The Lifting Bridge guards the entrance to the museum arm and prevents boats being removed. The flat deck of the bridge makes it easier for vehicles to cross the canal than if a fixed humpback bridge were used.*

LEFT: *Many of the buildings in the Boatdock have been built from redundant boats and their timbers. They still provide adequate working space for the Boatbuilder.*

TOP: *The massive wall of the 1842 Lime Kilns towers over the end of the canal arm.*

ABOVE: *The entrance to Dudley Canal Tunnel does little to suggest that it provides access to the fascinating Castle Mill Basin and the spectacular underground Limestone Caverns.*

RIGHT: *The Black Country canal system was linked to the waterways throughout England. Canal boats brought cargoes here from Gloucester or Ellesmere Port.*

The role of the Black Country Living Museum, a charity, has not changed since 1975 but the scope of the collections and the breadth of the displays continue to expand as it develops as the leading regional cultural heritage centre and major visitor attraction.

For more than 30 years buildings have been rescued, rebuilt on site and brought to life with furniture, fittings and welcoming costumed demonstrators. Each new development has attracted more visitors – almost 300,000 in 2008 – and the income generated has allowed us to expand the collection and preservation of material relating to the history of the Black Country and to carry out research into the unique history of the very heart of industrial Britain.

In 2000, the opening of the museum entrance complex, originally built as a public baths in Rolfe Street, Smethwick, some eight miles from the museum, provided stores for the collections not on display. It houses research and archive facilities, function rooms and two major exhibition halls: 'Introducing the Black Country' explains where the Black Country is and what it is famous for, while in 2009 a new display, 'The Museum: The Heart of the Black Country,' provides information which cannot be made available on site and sets the open air displays in the wider context of the development of the region.

ABOVE: *The Exhibition Hall.*

LEFT: *Rolfe Street Baths.*

BELOW LEFT: *Broome's Garage.*

BELOW CENTRE: *Fish tile in Hobbs fish and chip shop.*

BELOW: *Black Country Motor Co. Ltd.*

In 2006, the £10 million 'Streets Ahead' campaign was launched to move the museum to a new level with unrivalled standards of authenticity, excellent collections care, better accessibility, greater community involvement and improved sustainability. Its success can already be seen not only in the Cradley Heath Workers' Institute of 1912, Folkes Park and the new Rolfe Street exhibition but also in the Black Country Motor Co. Ltd where many of the museum's locally built cars and motorcycles are displayed, and Alex Broome's 1930s motor garage.